Dear Mom

Letters to Our Mothers

**compiled by:
Vanessa Canteberry**

Copyright @2019 by Vanessa Canteberry

All rights reserved. No part of this publication may be reproduced, stored in a retrieval system, or transmitted in any form or by any means electronic, mechanical, photocopying, recording, or otherwise without the written permission of the authors.

Limits of Liability-Disclaimer

The authors and publisher shall not be liable for your misuse of this material. The purpose of this book is to educate and empower. The authors and/or publisher do not guarantee that anyone following these techniques, suggestions, tips, ideas, and/or strategies will become successful.

The authors and/or publisher shall have neither liability nor responsibility to anyone with respect to any loss or damage caused or alleged to be caused directly or indirectly by the information contained in this book.

Table of Contents

Dedication i

Introduction..1

Chapter 1: The Angel That Gave Me
My Confidence......................................5

Chapter 2: Become A Better Daughter...............22

Chapter 3: Becoming My Greatest Me...............39

Chapter 4: Because You Love Me 55

Chapter 5: You Are Appreciated 65

Chapter 6: Am I Becoming My Mother?...........74

Chapter 7: Growing Pains..................................102

Chapter 8: Feeding the Ducks 113

Chapter 9: Carrying the Paton 120

Acknowledgment..129

Dedication

This book is dedicated to the mothers who fought the mighty fight of making the best decision, who remained open to being better in raising children regardless of the situation. Too often we have single mothers who have to play dual roles, deal with sleepless nights, and even work multiple jobs in order to make sure there is food on the table. Many times you wanted to walk away, but you stayed and accepted the challenges in life and did the best you could and always looked for ways to make it better. We thank and appreciate you.

For the mothers who did know how to be a mother and walked away from their children; sometimes, being in the home but not being 'present' could lead down a road of devastation. We have to be willing to do what is in the best interest of the child but at the same time; do not become a repeat offender.

Regardless of the situation, we need our mothers to love, nurture, and guide us.

Thank you to the mothers who stepped in to take part in molding the next generation. Sometimes you don't have to be the birth mother to be a mother. We appreciate you for loving us when we didn't feel loved. When we cried, you dried our eyes and reassured us, "Everything will be all right."

Being a mother is one of the hardest, unappreciated, and at times unrecognized duties, but when the role is switched, we get it. We appreciate you even more for your sacrifice and dedication.

Love always,

Your child

Introduction

Your heartbeat is the first sound we hear while in your womb. We are connected to your emotions throughout the pregnancy. We know your voice before we are even born. You feel our movements when we are hungry, not feeling well, or just trying to get comfortable. Your body stretched and even left some marks, but you birthed a miracle, and for that alone, we thank you.

Moms experience a lot with their bodies just to carry us and then carry the world on their shoulders just to make sure we are okay. They get up and take charge of various situations because they are often told they have to remain strong, as the woman is the core that holds the family together. They always make sure homework is done, the house is cleaned and food is on the table. They often find themselves putting out fires in between chaos.

However, what happens when the mom walks away and decides that she doesn't want to be a mom and/or doesn't know how to mother a child? We question the mother as if she decides to change her mind to be a parent, yet allowing her to marinate with her decision. It's like allowing them to flip the coin to choose whether they want to be a parent or not, but we will jump all over the father if he thought of walking away. We will pass the ball just enough, hoping you catch it, but if you don't, then there is always a next time.

Unfortunately, we have mothers who walk away from being a parent and it hurts. However, reading these stories from these amazing authors will give you a bright look into the importance of not only your presence as a mom but also your guidance that we need. Creating long-lasting memories that can be passed down to the next generation. From cooking meals in the kitchen to even passing down family recipes that no one could figure out the secret ingredient.

When tough love was necessary, and we didn't realize it, it hurt you more because you had to play the bad parent for a reason.

Taking a stroll down memory lane, we remember the words of wisdom you provided us, which we now can hold onto when we sit and think about the moments we needed to have a serious conversation about life and the reality of change. That type of uncomfortable conversation we thought didn't matter until the moment we had a collision with life. The conversation keeps us going when we want to stop.

We need you not only to raise us but to guide us when we need it the most without you even saying a word. It seems like you know what we were thinking before we even say it. You knew the person we were dating was not the right one for us but respected it because you knew we would eventually wake up from the clouds and come back to reality.

The moments of creating new memories with your grandchildren and experiencing the joys of you allowing them to get away with things we, your children, would never think of. You spoiling them just enough with the fullness of love, laughter, and of energy. Memories that cannot be erased. Now, that's precious, but unfortunately, everybody doesn't get to experience that side. But reading the transparency of these stories will give hope to the hopeless in knowing that we are not perfect but perfect enough to be loved in a way sometimes we just may never understand.

We hope you enjoy these amazing stories from the authors and their relationship with their moms.

The Angel That Gave Me My Confidence to Go Forward

By:
Michael Wynn

Dear Mama,

Thank you for all the lessons I learned growing up. Because of you, I developed a strong self-image. On May 8, 2007, as I sat quietly in your hospital room where you lay looking like an angel sleeping, I took a moment to reminisce about the many things you would say in the love of.

So, Mama, now that I can't hear the words physically coming from your mouth because of your transition, I thought about the many characteristics you said you admired in me, like my confidence and my willingness to help others. Your support directed me to act right and to be good to myself and others, no matter what the environment was. I learned how to live a peaceful life, and I was determined to take some pages from your life story.

You would always say, "Things happen for a reason" and "Worrying is a needless occupation"; these quotes continue to be my pick-me-up to this day. This statement gave me the strength to continue whatever I started. Through my life journey and through growing up, you always made sure to give me a thought, a prayer, or advice on a habit that I should pay attention to. Even in your peace, I know I will always hear your voice telling me, "Always keep prayer first."

Thank you, Mama, for caring for our family. Even at an early age, I recognized the love and support you gave to each of us but for me, the confidence, dignity, morals, self-respect, and self-assurance that I needed for my self-image.

So, Mama, you understood my journey as your third oldest child, along with Sandy, Calvin, Fredrick, Charlette, Sharon, and Gregory. Because it was really hard for me, since I *was* your favorite child, at least that is what I had to keep reminding the others since you named me after Michael the "Angel." Although you would often tell us, "Each one of you is my favorite child," I'm sure you had to say that to them to keep them emotionally balanced so we could continue to enjoy the many fun times that we had.

It was not all that bad growing up in a family many called 'poor.' Because of you, we lived in a happy, clean household that was very rich in spirit, and we had lots of fun. In fact, as children, we never knew what poor was until we got older. However, it was different living just down the street from Mama Hushie. I saw the connection between you and your mother, as you were her only child. Mama Hushie was truly that stern lady, one of six girls from Star City, Arkansas. You warned us that she didn't put up with any mess, and I found that out many times over and over again when I got in trouble.

Although you and Dad had many struggles raising us, you always managed to have a big smile on your face. Even when you had to help make ends meet by getting a job as a cashier at the King Cole Super Market a few blocks away, you would still show your passion like you were that stay-at-home mom who wanted to watch and care for us as we grew up. And I finally got what you meant when you would say, "Real people don't have to prove it."

Because I was an active and happy child who expected a lot of attention, I remember when I had to create some drama just to be in the middle of the action. And when I got tired of that drama, I would sneak into Mama Hushie's living room to stand near the bay window without touching anything so I could see you walking down the street from work in your King Cole uniform, with bags in your hands. The sight of you was exciting for me because your self-image and pride always radiated from your face, no matter what. Since we didn't have a car, we had to take the bus, or Mama Hushie had to drive us around if we had to go far. Because of this lack, we always had to get up very early for church or spend a lot of time with Mama Hushie during her shopping sprees at her favorite spots in

Hamtramck and downtown Detroit. But I remember going and hearing your voice in the background about how we better behave.

You brought so much clarity to many different situations. When we later moved from Clairmont to Martindale Street, I remember when I saw Daddy coming home from work in his stained overalls as a 'garbage man' while I was playing in the street with my friends. I remember telling you how sometimes I would feel embarrassed because my friends would make fun of us. Although Daddy did not have much time to play with us, I was still happy to see him. So, you told me I wouldn't fix that feeling of embarrassment until I asked him about his job. I did, and he said to me with a smile, "The pride I have in having a job is a job you can count on, and this is why you work hard, so people can talk about you."

Another time was when you asked me to go to the store with you, and I felt really special. I remember before going to the supermarket, I had to get the two-wheeled folding shopping cart out while you got your shopping list together. During any such outing, you always reminded us about your expectations for our behavior, manners, and patience. You had your sayings, like "Your habits show who you are, and they don't lie" and "Trouble is easy to get into but hard to get out of." Since I was so excited about just being out, I nodded my head like I was really listening to you. However, I actually missed out on what you meant about habits and trouble; I blatantly ignored a nugget of your wisdom. I felt like you gave me the freedom to go shopping.

As I walked up and down the wide aisles, avoiding the wet floors near the yellow caution signs, my excitement really began to show. I pushed the shopping cart, bobbing my head like I was doing the shopping, as I checked out my favorite junk foods lined down both sides of the aisles. I remember thinking to myself, *I can't wait to get my treat for helping you.* As I tried dropping a few hints, you kept looking away at your grocery list to make sure that you got everything. I thought that would be the best time to ask you for a chunky candy bar, and I remember you telling me "No!" because you were making us dessert. I remember failing one of your rules on behavior, so I was not ready to hear a "No" from you, especially since I felt like I *should* get a reward. I regretted the disappointment of waiting until you looked away, as I stuck the candy in my shirt pocket. Feeling entitled then, I still remember the guilt that I had as I gripped the candy bar and held onto it, with my right hand crossed over my chest to the left side of my shirt pocket. I acted like you were unaware of this candy, as I tried to help you load the bags into the shopping cart using only my left hand, lifting one bag at a time.

I just *knew* I had gotten away with something, but shortly after we got home, you asked me to take the bags in the house and then come and explain what was in my shirt pocket. Looking confused, I wasn't sure what to say, so I remember lying to you right away, "The man in the store said it was okay."

I can still hear your reply, "What man? And why would he say it's okay to steal?" Still holding onto my pocket, I started tearing up and said, "I don't know. Because I was being good, I think." But with that angry look on your face, you said, "Boy, be truthful." And before you could start the next sentence, I remember saying, "But Mama, I was really being good, so how come I couldn't have a treat?" And you said, "Because I said so. But you would lie to me and steal a candy bar to make matters even worse!"

I remember crying a little to show you sorrow and remorse, thinking maybe there was a chance of getting out of a whipping. But that acting scene didn't convince you enough because once you started lecturing me about your disappointment, I knew it was a done deal that I was going to get a whipping.

While standing there in dread of the punishment, I watched you sit down in one of the brown chairs in the living room and start to put on your shoes. Not knowing what to say, I stood in silence, watching you. When you finished, you stood and said, "Let's go." You walked to the door and yelled back to Sandy, letting him know that we were going back to the store. It was the most uncomfortable time I ever spent with you, as we walked all the way back to the supermarket, a few blocks away. That day, however, the walk seemed like a mile, as I watched the sweat run down the side of your face, and I studied your look of disappointment. You never said a word while we walked back to the store. But once we got to the store, I saw your beautiful and polite spirit appear, the one you always preached about to us, that we should always put on our best regardless.

As you calmly asked for the store manager, I remember being scared and embarrassed as you explained to him that I took a candy bar without paying for it. However, while you were looking toward him, I remember your voice penetrating throughout the store: "There would be no stealing in my family. My son has something to say to you." I just stood there, thinking, *If I get out of this alive, I will never steal again.*

You then said in a stern tone, "Michael, what do you have to say about that candy bar?"

I looked up at that tall, slim man wearing a green-striped apron as he waited patiently. I remorsefully said, "I just want to say I am sorry for stealing the candy bar and making my mama mad at me for stealing. I will never do anything like this again."

Well, not only did you make me give that candy bar back, but you also offered me up to the store manager to work for weekends, cleaning up around the store with no pay. But I was really lucky because the store manager said, "That is a nice gesture, but because of his age, the store policy won't allow him to work at the store, even if it is for free."

So, instead, you made me write a letter of apology that I had to later read to Mama Hushie before giving it to the store manager. Once we got home, I tried to sneak in without talking to anyone, but you called me into the kitchen. As I walked in, I pushed the swinging door, closing it so Sandy and Calvin couldn't hear us talking. You made me put up the groceries while you lectured me even more and reminded me about the whipping that I was going to get.

After I got my whipping, and right before bedtime, I still felt like I had really disappointed you. I looked in your room and saw you lying in the bed with both nightstand lights on, as you were reading your Bible. Before I could say anything, it was just like you smiled and gave me some words of comfort, as you reminded me why I got that whipping. You then explained the importance of learning my lesson because you refused to have a crook or thief living in our house. You told me to hold my head up so we can work on forgiving, forgetting, and moving forward. You quoted a verse from the Bible like you always did to prove a point.

You also made me read a Bible verse; it was from Colossians 3:13, as I remember my voice cracking, "Bear with each other and forgive one another, if any of you has a grievance against someone. Forgive as the Lord forgave you." After I finished reading, we said a prayer, and I felt a sense of relief. I cherished that moment because you always told us about having a visual of faith with a can-do-better spirit. Your forgiveness gave me a great moment of knowing that I had another chance to prove my honesty and love to you in return.

I remember when we moved again this time, to Ohio Street, where we planted our roots at least until I finished high school. Since Sharon was born just after we moved, and Gregory born two years later, I remember how you expected us to watch over them and guide them to doing what was right. It seemed like everything in this neighborhood was just too close for comfort; it was hard to have any real fun without getting in trouble. Like living down the street from the convent of St. Brigid Roman Catholic Church, where the nuns lived, you had the nuns on watch. And since our elementary school was only four blocks away, it didn't take much for you to quickly get there if you had to. But it was when you decided to go back to work, and you took a job in the lunchroom. The kids just loved you because of your beautiful smile, and they called you the 'Lunchroom Lady,' which made me jealous sometimes because you would remember their names as they made out to be your kids as well. However, the teachers and staff called you Mrs. Wynn, especially when they were ready to report to you if any of us acted up.

Because we lived in an integrated neighborhood, you taught us to learn how to understand all people. So, we managed to have some great fun with our neighbors who lived on our block.

However, there were some hateful and not-so-friendly neighbors who lived behind us, across the alley. You were the most authentic person I knew because you always faced reality, even with boundaries. You taught us not to judge people based on the way they looked, especially by the color of their skin. As kids, however, we sometimes fell short in defending ourselves from people using racially-motivated words toward us, thinking that most people we crossed were good people who were just being funny.

You would always tell us about having confidence in ourselves as you gave us teachable moments to grow up being positive. And Mama, I remember how you shared that understanding to me and Calvin during the winter of 1965, shortly after we moved in, while playing outside, making snow angels and a crooked snowman, who was so cool, with a mixture of snow, grass, and dead leaves for an outfit. However, the cold weather didn't bother us nearly as much as the frigid attitude that came from a white man who lived behind us. He saw us, and as he walked up to close his gate, I remember he made some racial slurs in which, at that time, at the ages of 9 and 10, we thought he was just making conversation, as we answered back in a happy voice, being naïve, with no concerns of what he said. So, when you saw us talking to that man and later asked us what that was about, and after we told you in his same words as if we accepted the title that he gave us, I remember the stern look on your face as you processed that information. Then you took a pause and asked us, "Do you love yourself?"

We solemnly said, "Yes."

I remember you saying, "You are two good-looking boys, and you're Negros. However, sometimes, jealous or wicked people will call you out of your name to make you unhappy or test your weakness for violence." I remember you telling us to defend ourselves by not letting evil words get in the way of what we stood for. If we love ourselves fully, we should focus on the good that's around us, and everything would be all right.

Mama, you made it easy for all of us to learn and have fun at the same time because of your spirit of enjoying life. And as teenagers, although we had to adjust to the shame of not having a car and not being able to do as much as our friends, we later learned how to turn our misfortunes into special times because during Christmas, there were many times we went without gifts, as we didn't have much money to buy gifts. But despite that, we still found ways to have fun sharing gifts with each other, as we would wrap an old toy in comic paper and gift them to each other.

You always encouraged us to be real and to know ourselves, especially while living in this big world with so many people and opinions. You really taught me to live my authentic life from the time I woke up and to always be true to myself and forgive and forget. From a teenager into manhood, I really learned how to grow from all your lessons, and I thank you so much for being there to help me with my confidence and self-image. Mama, for the rest of my life, I will always cherish the love and guidance that you gave me.

ABOUT THE AUTHOR

Michael Wynn from Detroit, MI, is the Owner of Coach "Win", LLC. As a Habit Success Strategist, Speaker and Best-Selling Author, Michael uses his 30 plus years of experience in financial compliance, business management and personal training to coach and provide valuable advice on optimizing with habits. Michael's careers include State of Michigan Departments of Transportation, Treasury, and Education; the Detroit Public Schools; Labor Unions; Construction Companies, Accounting, and Law Firms.

Michael is also Certified as an Authenticity Coach; Certified Financial Literacy Trainer, Certified Fraud Examiner, and Licensed Builder. As a proud recipient of an Outstanding Financial Literacy Award from the Michigan Accounting Aid Society, Michael was recruited as a contributing author for a former Detroit based newspaper, The Michigan Citizen, to write " Motivational" and "Focus Financial Literacy" articles. He is currently a contributing author for his church newsletter The Informer.

Michael wrote a best-selling book called "Habits Don't Lie!, 7 Habits To Overcome Obstacles To Win, and he uses his authentic voice as he gives thought-provoking, entertaining, and motivational support to his audience. Michael's ability to overcome a bi-polar and depression disorder with habits uniquely qualifies him to provide creative solutions to overcome obstacles. Michael enjoys the value of spending time with his wife Joyce, their children, grandchildren, and families. For more information, go to www.michaelwynn.com

Also, feel free to stay connected on Social Media with Michael Wynn at:

https://www.facebook.com/michaelwynnLive
https://www.instagram.com/coachmikewins
https://twitter.com/michaelwynnLive
https://www.linkedin.com/in/michael-wynn

Become A Better Daughter

By:
Marlo Grandberry

Dear Mom,

Every time I see you, I am reminded of how precious it is to be in your presence. Watching you smile, laugh, and enjoy yourself fills my heart with joy. I want to take more pictures, capturing the moments, and focus more energy toward creating new memories with you.

I haven't always felt this way about you. Regrettably, I now understand how much I took you for granted. I have always loved and valued you, but I took for granted that I would always have you in my life. I took for granted that there would be time available to spend with you at my convenience. It wasn't until the fall of 2018 that I felt the fear of losing you with great intensity.

There was something in your voice that prompted a sense of urgency for me to get home to see you. Your conversation had a tone of defeat and fatigue. All I knew was that I needed to see you as soon as possible! When I flew home for four days in October, I was reminded of how deeply connected we are, even though we live over 600–700 miles apart. Just because we barely speak twice a month and sometimes only see one another twice a year, our spirits have a way of syncing when we spend time together.

Perhaps, as I mature, I am becoming more aware of the time. I now have a better understanding of just how precious life is because of what happened earlier in the year. In April of 2018, I lost several co-workers within the same month. All of them were younger than you and Daddy. Two were men that were sickly. I was aware of their frequent visits to the hospital. The other co-worker I only saw periodically had kept her cancer and chemotherapy a secret. The day I found out she was placed on hospice, was Friday, April 6th, 2018. I left work early to visit her. I coordinated meeting two other colleagues so we could visit her together. We were en route shortly after noon when her daughter called to cancel our visit. We were blocks away when she passed away, and the family no longer wanted visitors.

Instead of driving home, we stopped at a Wendy's restaurant to talk, cry, and sulk with our comfort food, the infamous Frosty. As we talked, we reminisced about the great memories we had created over the years. We laughed, and we cried. We discussed how much we wanted to tell her we loved, valued, and appreciated her. It seemed as though we were attending funerals of co-workers from DLA (Defense Logistics Agency) quite frequently. The funerals for Dumas and Sarah were within weeks of one another in November and December 2016.

The very next morning, April 7th, I received a call that my buddy Mr. Burnes had passed away. A week prior, he informed me that he was being released from the hospital and placed on hospice, with stage four cancer. I spoke to him several times, but he canceled our attempts for me to visit. Even though he said he was on hospice, I thought we would have weeks or a month. I never imagined hospice equated to a few days. Oh, how precious time is, yet we take it for granted every day. Mr. Burnes was my buddy! He had a laugh that was contagious and filled with a healthy joy of life. I will always remember how much he loved his music. Before he retired, I called his office the 'Juke Joint.' I didn't know him long, only about 3 years. Nevertheless, the quality and depth of our conversations created a strong bond. Talking to him was like talking to a favorite uncle. He was just a cool dude, and I loved listening to him share life stories and nuggets of wisdom. When I told him about our trip to Atlanta, he told me he admired our relationship. I expressed my desire to be a better daughter for you. He told me to keep up the good work, and that is exactly what I intend to do.

On Monday, April 9th, I reported to work after a long weekend of sorrow and tears. I shared the heartbreaking news—that Mr. Burnes and Mrs. Haden both passed away on Friday with almost everyone. One of my co-workers was not at work. The week prior, Mr. Williams had a terrible cough. After being out for several days, my supervisor informed us that Mr. Williams was in the hospital again, and it wasn't looking good for him. The next week, he had passed away also. The loss was too much to bear in such a short time frame. Three funerals within one month was overwhelming! Everything was changing faster than I could process or adjust. One day, they were here; the next day, they were not.

Although I cried a lot and still have emotional moments, I realized the greatest thing that brought me sorrow was accepting that I would not be able to create any new memories with them. All of the memories I had were all I would ever have to remember them. Daddy was surprisingly sweet during this time. After I told him about losing three of my coworkers, he must have been worried about my wellbeing. He texted me several uplifting messages daily for a couple of weeks. I didn't know Daddy could be so sensitive. This was when I confronted myself about every relationship in my life. I was not the best steward of the relationships I have with my family and friends. There was a lot of room for improvement, and being an introvert meant I had to make some major mental shifts. You, Mom, are at the top of my list! I wrote Daddy his letter of thanks and appreciation as a gift for his 70th birthday.

Thankfully, the Lord had placed a very special lady in my life that demonstrated the type of daughter I want to be for you. She is a former co-worker of mine, and I lovingly refer to her as my 'Work Mama.' Cindy would call her mother every day during her lunch break. She would also schedule two family vacations with her parents annually around their birthdays. Every year, she took her parents places they wanted to go. They wanted to visit other family members who weren't able to travel, and her mother enjoyed taking cruises. Over the years, we had many conversations regarding our differences in communicating with our mothers. She was a little older than I, and I valued all of her West Virginian wisdom. She would encourage me to call you more. I even set a reminder alarm on my mobile phone to call you every Monday afternoon. I wish I could say I consistently called whenever the alarm reminds me, but I don't. Regrettably, I still get distracted and forget to call at times; however, I try to text a quick message so you would know I was thinking of you. I am becoming a better daughter one step at a time.

When her mother was diagnosed with Alzheimer's, I witnessed how hard it was for Cindy to watch her mother deteriorate and prepare to lose her permanently. Logically, everyone knows that death is the final stage of life for everyone. However, grief is handled differently by everyone. Yes, she cried, but as her mother reached the final stages of Alzheimer's, Cindy was more concerned with her mother's peace and quality of life. Although Cindy misses her mother, she has lots of memories and pictures from their vacations to warm her heart and share with her grandchildren.

I have another friend that set a wonderful example of being a good daughter. Levenda and I have been friends since 1991. We met during our pregnancy with our sons. She always said she would retire and relocate to Texas so she could live closer to her parents. After living in Virginia her entire 20-year military career, she had missed numerous birthdays, anniversaries, and special events. She often shared that she wanted to be close enough to drive home to visit her parents on the weekends, and she did. She also spoke to her mother every day. When her mother passed away in 2017, Levenda had no regrets. She honored and appreciated her mother while she was able to do so.

Mom, these ladies inspired our first trip as adults in August 2009. It was our *girls' trip*. Levenda and I wanted to take you and her mom, Ms. Minnie, to Las Vegas. We wanted you two to meet since you both loved playing slot machines. Although I did not understand the enjoyment of playing the slot machines, I enjoyed watching you enjoy yourself. You two played a long time on the nickel slot machines. I enjoyed our morning conversations as we drank coffee and tea. It was nice having you all to myself. This is what Cindy was encouraging me to do. She wanted me to get to know you as a woman and see you as a woman and not just my mother.

My Most Memorable Childhood Moments

Growing up, I did not want to be like you. Please don't get offended. I thought you were too nice, especially to Daddy. You were quiet and passive. I viewed these traits as weaknesses because you wouldn't stand up for yourself. Aunt Debbie and Aunt Pat were very vocal and expressed themselves unapologetically with confidence, boldness, and sassiness. Daddy's words would often be sharp and harsh, and you would just carry on as if he had said nothing. I recall asking you why you never snapped back at Daddy. Your response was simple and wise; you said, "It takes two to argue. If I stop talking, eventually he will too." Your refusal to engage in the argument was effective in de-escalating situations. Surprisingly, when I later learned to apply your wisdom stop talking to end arguments it worked for me too.

I believe I was around the age of 16 or 17 when my perspective of you changed forever. I recall standing in front of the stove, putting dinner away. Daddy was fussing at me about something as he entered the kitchen. Honestly, I was probably deliberately moving slow to do what I was supposed to do. That was my passive aggressive way of being rebellious. Well, whatever he said, it was exactly what I had anticipated him saying in my mind. As he passed behind me, I smirked. Internally, I was laughing and struggling to maintain my composure. I soon realized he saw me when he stepped back and slapped me on my right cheek. Hysterically, I started screaming, and the chicken flew up in the air as I ran in the bathroom. Mommy, I heard you come upstairs from the basement. Knowing you, you were washing clothes. You asked Daddy what was going on. After he told you he had slapped me, you went off. You told him this, that, and the other. I proudly lowered my whimper so I could hear every word. I didn't know you could be that tough. I remember staying in the bathroom for hours. I think my feelings were hurt more than anything. I had never been slapped in the face. Now that I think about it, I have never slapped anyone in the face. It is a degrading form of disrespect. Nevertheless, I learned that day that I could always count on you to come to my rescue.

Good mothers protect their children. Your 'Mama Bear' protective instincts reassured me that your strength was not in your words but in your presence. When the situation called for it, you released a mighty roar.

Another memorable moment was when you grounded me the summer after I graduated. That July, I had thrown a party for my friend Damita. We were underage and had been drinking. Being the responsible one in my group, I decided to call you. I wanted you to know I had been drinking, and I was NOT going to drive home. Your response was calm, cool, and collected; you said, "Okay." I remember bragging all night about how proud you were of me for not drinking and driving. So, imagine how shocked I was when I walked in the door the following afternoon, and you were angry with me. I didn't understand why you were so angry but didn't get angry when I called the night before. You grounded me for two weeks, only permitting me to go to work.

I complained to one of my co-workers that I was grown, and it was crazy for you to ground me. After all, I was finished with high school and preparing to go away to college. My coworker would laugh and mock me, saying, "You better take your grown tail straight home after work." After several days of listening to him encourage me to talk to you, I finally did. When I asked you why you grounded me after I had called you, you simply said, "You had never done anything like that before, and I expected you would be home later, but you came home the next afternoon." You also disclosed that Daddy was instigating and encouraging you to pack my clothes and put them on the porch. After our conversation, you let me off of punishment a week early. You told me some things I would not understand until I had children of my own. I am so thankful for our ability to communicate. Now, I understand the worry of a mother to want to protect her children from a dangerous and evil world.

YOUR LEGACY

Mom, I don't recall many interactions between you and Grandma Josephine. However, I modeled my parenting from your values and added a few of my own. I watch you as a grandmother to my seven nieces and nephews, and you continue to be a pillar of love, acceptance, and consistency, just like you were with my sons. Now that I am a grandmother, and you are a great grandmother, I am more determined to ensure we take more pictures, plan more vacations, and create more memories. I am mentally preparing stories to tell your great grandson about you.

As I matured and became a wife and mother, I have learned that it takes a great deal of strength and self-control to maintain one's peace, especially when circumstances and people try one's patience. Your consistent loving and encouraging demeanor has been a foundation in my life, enabling me to continuously strive to new heights. Mom, I need you. You, my children, and my grandson, MJ are why I continue to push myself to be the best version of myself. I want you all to be proud of me.

THANK YOU

I am so thankful that you are alive and I have the opportunity to tell you how much I appreciate you. You may have a few aches and pains here and there, but you can handle it. I have several aches and pains myself. Now that you are in your 70s, it is extremely important for you to keep moving. Recently, I was listening to the news, and I heard a gentleman say, "Exercise should be a celebration of what you can do, not a punishment for what you ate." Mom, I wish you would take this perspective. Focus on what works well for you. Take a dance class, water aerobics, or join a walking group. Celebrate your mobility! I need you for at least another 20–30 years. So, keep moving, Mommy!

Lastly, I need you to dream again. Please make a wish list of places you would like to go and things you would like to do. If not now, then when? Several of my friends no longer have the opportunity to create new memories with their mothers. I told Karen, my bestie for over 30 years, that she could always call you when she needs a 'Mommie' hug. I don't know how it feels to not have you, and I am not in a hurry to find out just how hard life would be without you. I love you, Mom, and I want the world to know how much of an honor it is for me to be your daughter.

My Declaration to You, Gloria D. Grandberry

I declare I will spoil you to the best of my ability. I want you to know how much I love you by showing you through word and deed.

I declare we will take at least one trip or vacation annually. It would really help if you create a list. It is never too late for dreams to come true.

I declare I will retire you so you can enjoy the freedom of creating your own schedule.

I declare I will call or text at least once a week consistently.

I declare I will continue to become the best daughter possible because you are the best Mom ever!

ABOUT THE AUTHOR

Ms. Marlo M. Grandberry was born and raised in the Detroit metropolitan area of Michigan. She graduated from high school in 1988 and attended Michigan State University in East Lansing, Michigan. After her freshman year, she joined the military to "see the world." Her Naval career as a storekeeper, also known as a logistics specialist, began the summer of 1989.

During her 21-year career, she was assigned to many duty stations in Norfolk, Virginia. She served on three ships and two shore commands. In 1999, she decided to continue her career and retire from the Navy Reserves in 2010. The military helped her discover and develop into a confident and competent woman, leader, and entrepreneur.

Marlo is the daughter of Mr. & Mrs. Melvin and Gloria Grandberry. She is the mother of two sons, Maurice and Dimetrius. Thanks to her lovely daughter-in-law, Skyla; she is a proud new grandmother, lovingly referred to as 'Nana,' to the cutest fella imaginable, Maurice, Jr. Marlo only has one younger sister, Kristal, who has filled her heart with the joy of being an auntie to seven nieces and nephews, with the help of her husband, Darryn. Dylan, Layla Kassius, Madison, Able, Errol, and Chase have their special 'love names' with their auntie Marlo.

Marlo is intentional about her growth personally, professionally, and spiritually. She believes God intends for all of us to live and experience the abundance of life and encourages others to "see their cups as half full" and being filled to overflow. As a first-time published author, she is overjoyed to be able to honor her mother publicly in *Dear Mom*.

Feel free to stay connected with Marlo Granberry on Social Media at:

MsMGrandberry@gmail.com
www.facebook.com.MsMGrandberry
www.Instagram.com/marlograndberry
www.Linkedin.com/in/mgrandberry

Becoming My Greatest Me

By:
Dr. Pamela Caldwell

Dear Mom,

Where do I begin talking about our relationship and what it means to me and how it has helped me 'Become My Greatest Me'? I guess I will start at the present moment and say thank you for your support in the move to China, to the other side of the Pacific, on my own. I know it is hard on you, especially with the events that happened prior, but when I told you I was still going because that's what Dad would have wanted me to do, you didn't say a word; you supported me. Even when I started having doubts, you reminded me of why I was doing it. To this day, I cannot tell you how much I appreciate that. I know you worry about me because I have never been this far from you. You know what you tell me: "The one that was always up under me is now the furthest one from me. I just can't believe it." Trust me when I tell you God knew what I needed. He knew the events that I would have to go through before getting here. He knew, and He prepared the journey for me. You and Dad always told me to put my trust in God, and everything else will fall in line. So, that is what I did, and that has made all the difference. This journey that I am on, I am Becoming, I am Being, and I am learning how to Sustain My Greatest Me. I wouldn't have this experience if it wasn't for you and Dad. I know this book is titled *Dear Mom*; however, I cannot talk about our relationship without talking about Dad. The reason: it was that relationship that you had with my dad that allowed us to have the relationship that we have. Because Dad loved you and supported you, that gave you time and energy to love and support me. So, I can't talk about our relationship without talking about Dad. This letter will be about our relationship, with Dad thrown in the mix.

Where do I begin? I guess 9 months before January 29, 1975, when God decided that the world needed a Dr. Pamela Kay Caldwell in the mix. I know He knew how awesome I would be and what great things I would accomplish, and He knew He couldn't just have anyone be my mom and dad. He had fixed these years before you and Dad met. And He had to give you some practice, so that is why I am number 9. Oh my, my siblings are going to be mad when they read this, but it is our little secret; I am not telling anyone. Anyway, back to the letter. So, God searched high and low to find the perfect parents for this child that would one day become Dr. Pamela Kay Caldwell. He decided on Marion and Anna Caldwell; for that, I am grateful. Because of that, I am Becoming My Greatest Me Version Changchun.

Sometimes I sit, and I can barely believe I live in China for the school year. Not only that, but I am thriving. Can you believe that I am this far away from you? I remember a time when you couldn't go into the next room without me throwing a fit. I was serious about my momma and her location. Somedays, I think of all those attachment moments, and I just laugh. If someone would have told me that one day I would live on the other side of the ocean from my mom, I would have laughed and told them, "Never would I ever be that far away from my momma." Like you used to tell me, never say never. When you let God order your steps, anything is possible. I am living proof of that.

I guess I need to start at the beginning of our relationship so that the reader will know and understand our relationship now. We have always had a good relationship; I can never remember a time when we didn't have one. Like I have mentioned before, yes, this is *Dear Mom*; however, a lot of our relationship has to do with your relationship with Dad because he loved, cherished, respected, adored, and a lot of other adjectives that allowed you to Be Your Greatest You so that you could have a relationship with your children. You had 9 of us, and that was 9 individual relationships that you were able to have. You knew all of us like the back of your hand; we couldn't do anything without you knowing before we did it. To this day, I still don't know how you did it or if you had spies that we did not know about, and I am sure you will never tell me. That is okay; I have made up my own story of how you did it. Even though there were 9 of us, and you had 9 different relationships with us, I know mine was your favorite, but shh ... don't tell the others; you know how sensitive they can be. LOL (laugh out loud).

Where do I start? I guess like when we talk in person with stories, with no particular order; just remembering stories. You remember when I started kindergarten and barely got in because I was so not into talking to anyone that wasn't you, Dad, or my siblings. The teacher had you tell me what to do, and then I did it, and I told you. Then in first grade, my teacher thought I couldn't read. To my defense, it wasn't my fault; if she wanted me to read, all she had to do was ask me. No, she made it sound like it was an option for me to read, and you know if it was an option, then I didn't have to do it, and usually, I didn't, depending on my mood. Of course, she then put me in the lowest reading group; didn't bother me. I knew I could read. It wasn't my fault that she didn't know I could read. Then she called our group up and was like, "OK, Pamela, when I get to you, you have to read. I need to know what level you are at."

"Okay, Teacher!" was my response. And when she got to me, she asked, "OK, I need you to read." I was like, "Okay"; then I read the book. The teacher was like, "You can read." I said, "Of course, my momma taught me." "Then why didn't you read before?" she asked. "Because you didn't ask me. You asked if we wanted to read, and I didn't want to read," I replied.

I know you remember because I was always like that. If I didn't want to do it, I didn't. If it was an option, then I thought about it, and if I didn't want to do it, I didn't. I know I was a mess back then. Man I am a mess now. Living life to my own beat. I know you wonder where I get it from. Well, that is easy you and Dad. You all taught me to be whoever and whatever I wanted to be. "If you believe you can do it, that is all that matters." I still live by those words, which is why I tell people, "Party of 1." It's not that I believe I do not need anyone in my life but that I don't need others to believe in me in order for me to believe in me. Party of 1.

Do you remember when I had to take speech therapy class? I hated those classes, but I am sure you know that although I am glad I went, they have made a huge difference. I think I had to go for 2–3 years. Remember what you used to tell me when I felt bad about going? "Don't worry; you're just like your momma. Your momma can't say some words either." We would just laugh, and then I would not worry about it. It was words that started with 'ch' and 'sh.' Would you believe those are the same sounds I have a problem with in learning Mandarin (Chinese)? All I do is remember what I was taught in class, and then I got it. Those speech classes did come in handy; thank you for making me go.

Do you remember when I could barely stand in front of a class of 20 and say a speech? Oh, I hated speaking in front of people. I guess God had other plans because, now, I stand in front of classes with 100 plus students and lecture for more than an hour without blinking an eye. Like you and Dad would tell me, "You never know where life is going to take you."

Another thing I am grateful for is that you taught

me to love reading. I can sit and read all day. It's like I become someone else, experience another world. With technology, I listen to books and have the same effect. So, thank you for teaching me to read and love it.

I could go on and on about the stories of me being me. Looking back, I know you probably wondered, *What is she doing? Why is she being so much?* Looking back, I didn't know myself. I guess I was just being me. I still have those same traits if I don't want to do it, then I don't. I don't run with the crowd; I do my own thing.

I think the one thing I will forever be grateful for is that you pushed me. You pushed your children to be and do more. When you were in high school and an adult, opportunities were limited in what African Americans could do. However, that didn't stop you from teaching us different. Encouraging us to decide what we wanted to do. You taught us about education. You and Dad would always tell us, "Education is power. If you want to go places and do things, education is the key." You were serious about school. We just had this conversation how you had us and our teachers on lockdown. We couldn't do anything but be right, LOL.

You were serious that school wasn't a place to play; school was serious business. Listening to the teachers was the only option we had. Looking back, I am grateful, because you and Dad were right education is power, and it has and will continue to take me places I never dreamed of. I teach this to my students to this day. I tell them like you told me, "Education, knowledge; once you have it, they can't take it away from you. It is yours to do whatever and become whatever you want." Yes, I tell my students here about you and Dad. I am sure you never thought college students in China would know about you, but they do.

I know I keep saying this, but I want you to know that I am Becoming My Greatest Me because you are Your Greatest You. That is the only way I was able to have the life and continue to have the life that I have. It is all because of you; it is all because of the relationship you had with Dad. I have said it before; I know this letter is titled *Dear Mom* and about the relationship I have with you. However, we have the relationship that we have because of the relationship you had with Dad. Because that was a loving and caring relationship, it allowed you to be Your Greatest You so that I could be My Greatest Me.

I do not think people know the impact it has on a child when their parents are in a loving relationship. I only remember a peaceful environment; no yelling, no cussing, no acting silly (like you would say). There were disagreements; we all have them. Why? Because we are all different. However, that didn't stop you from handling them in the best way without all the silliness. At the time, I am sure you didn't understand how much of an impact that would have on me. To this day, I do not like arguing with people. If we can't sit down and discuss and come up with a solution, then we really do need to check ourselves and see what we are really doing. I don't like to be around confusion. I get that from you. You and Dad were not about the 'cray cray' (craziness). I appreciate that so much because you miss out on life and the little things.

Because it is the little things that make life worth living. I appreciate the environment that you created for me to grow up in; it has made all the difference in the world.

I remember when I was younger, we didn't take many trips, but when we did, they were always amazing. Nothing fancy; just exploring something new. I have developed that in my adult life. Here in China, people probably think I travel a lot, but I don't. I take pleasure in going to the local market and having somewhat of a conversation with the locals. Seeing the farmer with his cart being pulled by his donkey coming to town to drop off vegetables, I wave and say, "Nǐ hǎo." I enjoy the short trips around the country to see life on this side of the Pacific. I have learned so much about myself and about the world. We are truly interconnected. I am so grateful I was given the opportunity. I have grown so much. Sometimes I wish I could call Dad and tell him all about it. However, he is no longer on this side of life. He knew I was about to come, and he was so excited. You remember what he would say when one of us did something new, "I never thought I would live to see the day." I know you still talk to him daily and have told him all my stories. I know you have probably told him, "I can't believe our baby is all the way over there." I can't believe it sometimes either. I just thank God for the experience.

I thought about writing about when we were in Tucson with Dad. I decided against it; that was our time and our story. I do not feel that this is the platform I want to share it on. Just know that I am glad I was able to spend those last days with you and Dad, doing what we always do watch Western, talk, and enjoy life. I will always have those memories with me. The last song I sang to Dad is "God is Love." Till the end, he believed; we believed.

To this day, I miss Dad so much. You both were my person. Always there, always supporting me. I miss that; however, I still have you as my person. Now I am creating a new normal or trying to. Some days are better than others. They just don't tell you that when you lose a parent, it leaves a hole that is never filled. You just have the memories that help you get to the next moment. I keep moving forward, trying to make the world a better place.

I know what you are saying now: "Man she has a lot to say!" Yes, I do. When it comes to how much you mean to me and how much you have impacted my life, I can go on for days. I just want you to know without a doubt that I am grateful for all the sacrifices that you made in order for me to have a better life. I remember you always told me that if I believed in me, and you believed in me, nothing else mattered. You would also tell me when I didn't believe in me that you still believed in me, and that was good enough. No matter what I did, you were always there; you always believed that I could Be My Greatest Me. You believed in my Becoming My Greatest Me. You believed that I could do anything that I put my mind to. You believing in me has got me through the tough times when I would doubt me, when I thought I wasn't worthy. I knew you never doubted me, and you always thought I was worthy. I want you to know that meant/means everything to me.

I just want you to know that I appreciate everything you have done and will do for me. There are not enough words on the planet to tell you how much I appreciate you, how much I love you.

Until next time, just know that I Am Becoming My Greatest Me because You Are Your Greatest You.

I love you, wǒ ài nǐ, 我爱你

Your baby, Dr. Pamela Kay Caldwell

ABOUT THE AUTHOR

Dr. Pamela Kay Caldwell holds a Doctorate of Management Concentration in Social and Environmental Sustainability; an Executive MBA from Colorado Technical University; and a Bachelor of Civil Technology, Construction Management from the University of Houston. Originally from Dover, Oklahoma, with 17 years spent in Houston, Texas. Currently, she resides in Changchun, China, Jilin Providence. Dr. Caldwell is a business professor at Jilin University Lambton College, a higher education institute that partners with several schools located in the United States and Canada. Dr. Caldwell teaches undergraduate business classes and graduation classes for an MBA—Health Care Administra-tion. Dr. Caldwell also teaches online.

Dr. Pamela Kay Caldwell also owns K-LO

Coaching. K-LO Coaching is a business/transition coaching business that helps individuals navigate life's transitions successfully using the concept Becoming, Being, and Sustaining. K-LO Coaching provides one-on-one coaching classes and owns the My Greatest Me product line.

Follow Dr. Pamela Kay Caldwell on social media:

www.Facebook.com/klocoaching
www.Facebook.com/groups/mygreatestme
www.instagram.com/klocoaching
www.linkedin.com/company/klocoaching
www.klocoaching.com
drcaldwell@klocoaching.com

Because You Love Me

By:
Dr. Aikyna Finch

Dear Mom,

When you are a child, you really don't think about the time that your parents are gone as sacrifices for you. All you know is that your parents are not at home. Then the time that they are home, they are tired or distracted, so they might as well be gone. This is the way I remember you for most of my childhood. While I was entertained by my great-grandmother and grandparents most of the time, I did wish that you were around more. You were at work, doing overtime so I could have all the things that you didn't have as a child. When you did have time, we went on vacations and had quality time, but I know now how much you had to work to make those things happen for us. This taught me drive and dedication to making things happen in my life because you always did. It also taught me to not judge a book by its cover. Perception is powerful, so it should be used wisely!

Eventually, my great-grandmother got sick, and in addition to taking care of me, you had to take care of her as well. You balanced it for a while, but soon, my great-grandmother had to go to the nursing home; then she left this world. Then three months later, my grandfather passed away. So, at this point, the two people that watched me the most were gone, and all that was left was my grandmother. I learned many things from my grandmother, but love and affection were not included on that list. I now realize that you missed both of them as much as I did, but you couldn't be sad in front of me. These were the two people that you went to for attention, and they were both gone within three months' time. I wish I could have been more supportive to you, but that was when we found out about my death phobia, so that was something else that you had to deal with on top of this. So, spending time with my grandmother helped with the process because she didn't baby me at all. I had to toughen up to deal with her.

I spent nights with my grandmother until I was 14 when you got a day shift and were able to be at home with me. During this time, your sewing started to pick up, and you were sewing all of the time that you were not at work. I was entering high school, and you knew the expenses were coming for sure. During this time entered the boyfriend. I had no use for him, but he is a part of the story anyhow. From age 15 to 16, he was there, and we tolerated each other because we knew neither one of us were leaving for the time being. Then at 16, you got laid off the job you had since I was 5 months old. It was horrible, and I didn't know what I was going to do about anything. I was getting ready to start my senior year of high school in a few months, and I knew I was going to need money. Luckily, I had just started working a month before, so I was making my own money. That job showed me how much I was like you. I stayed on that job for 10½ years, and I learned how to do what I needed to do to make things work. This was the turning point in my life from being the single child princess to having to work for what I wanted overnight. It was what I needed to start surviving in the world as an adult. It also showed me that I could adapt and not crumble under pressure. Thank you so much for the lesson.

A few months later, you found another job paying less money, working second shift. It was a job, and the bills were being paid, but you were so unhappy. To make ends meet, you started sewing even more. I noticed whenever you were not happy, you always turned to sewing. I guess sewing was your crutch like working was my crutch. About a year later, I finished high school, and a year after that, the boyfriend was gone. I believe this was the last straw in your life. You were done being unhappy. You were tired of working a job that you hated. You were tired of doing things that you didn't want to do. So, one day, you made the decision to step out on faith. You quit your job and started sewing full time. I didn't understand this move at first, but I did know that you needed to be happy. You were talented enough to make it work, so I decided to believe in you like you always believed in me.

You did have hard times, but you were doing what you loved, so you were in better spirits, and that made me happy.

Since you had been sewing for years, you had a good-sized clientele. Our house became your office. People were at the house all of the time. This was hard to get used to in the beginning because I was used to being by myself all of the time. Slowly, the business started picking up, and you had to move out of the house because it was not zoned for business. You found out that your brother's duplex was in the right zoning area, and you moved the business across town. Once the business was moved, it was time to make the move and get the paperwork in order. You enrolled in a class for small businesses and obtained the paperwork needed to be a full business in Tennessee. This was a proud moment for you. That was one thing about you; whatever needed to be done to make the dream work, you made it happen. You were always a great role model in that regard.

Once you moved into the shop, the clientele grew. You were constantly busy. I do not believe that you ever really had downtime. You were sewing around the clock, so you started staying at the shop and left me alone in the house. It was the best time of my life. I paid my utilities, bought groceries, and cooked for myself. I believe this was the time I realized that I was not domestic in any way. I did enough to survive. This lasted for about 3 years. Then one day, you decided to come home, and about a year or so after that, the business had to move into the house we were living in, and it is still there to this day. Almost twenty years later, and Sewin' 2 Please is still going strong today. You tried to retire from sewing after hand and back surgery, but you just cannot seem to stop. When you are creating a dress from scratch, embroidering scarves, or making doll dresses, you are in your purpose, and you just cannot give it up because it gives you life.

You are starting to slow down the business now because you are starting to decide to sew for pleasure and not for business. You are more focused on your health and mind. You are in love with the Keto diet and have lost 50 pounds to date. You are trying to motivate me to do the same. You are so supportive of my business ventures now. You keep me motivated to keep going when I get sad and feel discouraged because you have been there in your life. You show me the importance of having a strong unit of family and friends. You always give me extra attention because you know that you are all I have in the world.

Because you loved me, I am successful in my life on my own terms. I was able to get six degrees and was the first to receive a doctorate on both sides of my family. I was able to start two companies while becoming an international speaker and certified coach. You taught me to fight for what I want. You taught me to be better than the average or the expected. You taught me to accept people and situations for what they are and then strive for greater. I am so glad that you are my mother. Yes, my father is present now that I am grown, but you held it down through my childhood alone and never asked for any assistance from him. I am so glad that you are my friend as well. I love that you see me as an adult, and you can share things with me as an adult. I appreciate you as a person. We are different in our personalities, but we have many of the same traits, and we understand that about each other. The best way to sum up our relationship is, I am everything I am because you love me!

Your daughter,
Dr. Aikyna Delores Finch

ABOUT THE AUTHOR

Dr. Aikyna Finch is a podcaster, social media coach, and speaker. She is also a Forbes Coaches Council member. She coaches in the areas of empowerment, life, and social media at the individual and groups levels from her company Finch and Associates, LLC. She co-hosts the Motivate Social Podcast by her company Changing Minds Online. She speaks about Motivation, Education, and Social Media and avidly livestreams on these topics.

Dr. Aikyna Finch is an educator and author. She received a Doctorate in Management, MBA in Technology Management, and Executive MBA from Colorado Technical University. She has a Masters of Management in Marketing Management and Masters of Information Systems in Project Management from Strayer University and Bachelors in Aeronautical Technology in Industrial Electronics from the

School of Engineering of Tennessee State University. Her teaching disciplines include business, leadership, marketing, social media, and information systems at the graduate and undergraduate levels.

Dr. Aikyna Finch is the co-author of seven books and launched her first solo project, Motivation Ignited, in November of 2016. She is a contributor to the Huffington Post, Goalcast, Forbes, and Shine Now Magazine. She has been interviewed and featured on Huffington Post, Hello Beautiful, Women Speakers Association, and many others. Dr. Aikyna Finch has spoken on many platforms, including the Periscope Summit, Women In Leadership Summit, The Boldly Empowering Entrepreneurs Conference, The Business Vlog Summit, and many more!

Feel free to stay connected with Dr. Aikyna Finch on social media at:

www.Facebook.com/DrADFinch
www.Instgram.com/DrADFinch
www.Twitter.com/DrADFinch
www.Linkedin.com/in/DrADFinch
www.aikynafinch.com

You Are Appreciated

By:
Christina Burleson

My Dear Mom,

I now know what you went through as a parent now that I am a parent myself. I am sorry. I now understand why you were frustrated and even mad at times because I left a trail of clothes, shoes, toys, books, and anything else that I left lying around the house, not caring if I came home to a dirty house, but I knew you cared because you worked hard all day long to keep the house clean. I now understand, Mom, how it feels like trying to keep your sanity with trying to complete all of your chores and running errands with three kids who were constantly fighting with each other. I know every day you made sure we had what we needed for school;

you put everyone first, while you put yourself last.

I know how hard it was on you when Dad went to Korea twice in his Air Force career. The first time, you were taking care of three babies by yourself, getting up with us in the middle of the night to feed and change us. Cleaning up after our messes, not having the support you needed. The second time Dad went to Korea, I know it was tougher on you than the first time. The second time, you had three kids who would constantly fight and talk back to you, not wanting to help you out. I remember that one night when we were driving back from the Walmart in Warrensburg, MO, when that snow storm hit. You were driving very slowly down the highway when, all of a sudden, you drove over a patch of black ice, and the car started spinning out of control and almost went over a huge ravine. Right after the car stopped at the edge, I got out of the car, trying to help you push the car back onto the road. Thank goodness some stranger stopped his truck and helped us get the car back on the highway. When we started driving down the road again, I remember you saying, "God must have been with us then." I have always remembered that because, even though it was just us, you gave me hope that we were going to be all right, even if it was just the three of us while Dad was away for an entire year.

I get it now, Mom. I know now what it feels like to be unappreciated. To feel like you are invisible to the world. Working a full-time job, and then coming home to cook dinner for two children, making sure they have their homework done and getting them ready for the next day. I am so very sorry, for I never really knew how hard you worked, how you struggled at times, and how you went without. I now understand how every single day was about us, even at the times we were ungrateful to have clean clothes, a hot meal, and a clean house to come home to. You did this day after day, month after month, and year after year.

I know what it's like now to be a mom and have to tell my kids "No!" when they want something. I have a ten-year-old who tells me at times she hates me or that I am mean because she doesn't get her way. When she started saying her choice phrases, I used to take it to heart, but now, I don't because I know I am doing my job as a parent, making sure my kids are safe and protected and knowing where they are. My ten-year-old might not understand my reasons when I tell her "No" or even after I explain it to her, but I know one day she will get it. I know I never said "Thank you" often, but I am saying "Thank you" now for taking care of us kids.

I also want to thank you for helping me out before and after I got divorced. I was in an abusive relationship with a psychotic man who was financially, emotionally, and physically abusive toward me, and when I needed someone to listen to me about the hell he put me through, you were there when no one else was. It is funny how you find out who your true friends are when your life gets tough. I realize going through this divorce I had lost my self-confidence, and I was not the person I once was before I got married. The constant name-calling and the threats I endured took its toll on me. It was so bad at times that I did not want to be around anyone because I was told by my ex-husband how no one liked me and how everyone thought I was a joke. You have been an incredible gift of strength and hope. You have taught me that no matter how tough life gets, keep going and never give up because life will get better.

I also can't thank you and Dad enough for driving down to Gatlinburg, Tennessee, when I and the kids had to evacuate Panama City, Florida, to escape from Hurricane Michael. I will never forget how you were willing to take the kids back to Ohio so I could drive back down to Florida to survey the damage of what this horrific storm did. I had made my peace with the thought that the kids and I had probably lost everything. When I finally got back down to Florida and was able to see the house for myself, it was just as you said on the phone: "Everything would be all right. God will take care of you." And you know what? He did. Some people would call it luck or a miracle from the divine presence of God, but I know I was blessed that I did not lose one item.

I was very fortunate enough the kids were able to stay with their grandparents and spend actual quality time with them while I made several trips back and forth to Florida, trying to get the house fixed. I know I would not have been able to do what I needed to get done if you had not been there for us. You have taught me to never lose sight of the fighting spirit. And even though I have seen a lot of heartache throughout my life so far, I have learned to never lose that sense of hope. Because of you, I have been able to reshape myself into the person I am today. I am not afraid of standing up for myself; I am not scared to walk away from people who purposely stab me in the back. I know I can overcome anything that comes my way.

I am sorry I was not the perfect child growing up, but we all make mistakes and learn from them. Everything happens for a reason, whether we realize it or not. You made sure I had everything I needed and that I did not have to go without. I now realize how fortunate I was growing up, and now that I am a parent myself, I understand the tough decisions you had to make on my behalf, even if it wasn't the 'most popular.' Thank you for keeping me safe and showing me the true meaning of having that generosity of spirit because even though I am not well off, I know that there are other people who are dealing with far worse situations than what I have had to deal with. Because of you, I now realize it is better to give to people than receive. There is more to life than just being materialistic, and it is sad how most of today's generation live with that type of stigma.

Being a single mother is not easy, and I would rather work a full-time job and raise two children entirely on my own than be married to a man who only cares about himself. I know I still have a lot to learn, but it's OK; you no longer have to worry about me. I know that I can handle anything that comes my way. I hope you know how truly thankful I am for you being the mom you were to me growing up and the mom that you still are. I now understand what you went through because, most of the time, it is a thankless job, and people don't know this until they become a parent themselves. I hope you know that I love you to the moon and back.

ABOUT THE AUTHOR

Christina Burleson is an Airman currently serving in the United States Air Force. She was born into the military life and has never lived in a place for more than four years. As an active duty Airman, Christina has traveled the world, holding various jobs in several different career fields. As a divorced single mother of two daughters, Christina is breaking her silence on the domestic violence she experienced while married for over 10 years. She wants to educate people about the warning signs of domestic abuse and how to escape from an abusive relationship while encouraging people not to be afraid to come forward.

Christina, while still on active duty, is aspiring to be a leadership coach/consultant to help people find their passion and purpose in life.

Feel free to stay connected with Christina Burleson on social media at:

www.Facebook.com/christinaburleson
www.Linkedin.com/in/christinaburleson

Am I Becoming My Mother?

By:
Deidre Norville

Dear Mom,

My prayer is that you and those who read this are inspired, see the love and mercy of Jesus from my perspective and that those who need it can view the relationship of mother and daughter through the eyes of Christ!! I pray the miracle of Christ is present and illuminated through this story and that the light of love and hope fills those that need our God the most!

My belief was that the broken pieces of my life could never turn into anything worthy. I felt distressed about sharing such intimate details and was fearful of the harsh judgments in reference to my sharing my feelings and perspectives. The Lord knows I would rather write a book about anything else besides one of the bigger hidden places in my heart that coddled the intense relationship with one of the wisest, boldest and most beautiful women I first knew in this life—my mother!

I pondered on why our relationship is the way it is. My thoughts often included: *Why can't my mom just do this?* Or, *Why can't my mom just do that?* Or even further, *How come she can't have the same relationship with my daughter as she does with my son?* Or, *Why is she so controlling?* These thoughts would often ring throughout my thoughts day in and day out, always wanting and expecting more or something else from you because you are my mother.

As a mother of two myself, I totally understand that parenting doesn't come with an instruction manual, and I know you grew up in a time when for us as a black family, "things were not talked about, which in reality is keeping a secret." But in truth, and reflecting on my childhood, things were really intense. My childhood had turmoil, fear, depression, alcoholism, anger, and long periods of isolation which felt like abandonment.

Not to mention that to this day, I have never met my biological father, siblings, or anyone of that part of my paternal family. The thought process of keeping things hidden, not talking about them, and not being able to heal from them will stop with my family ... Sometimes our God is like that; He allows things to happen so He can do something bigger. So, because I survived it, it's part of my responsibility to solve the problem in our family. So, with the dominion and love that God gives me, I break this cycle for my family now in the name of Jesus!

I want you to know that it is only by the power of the Holy Spirit and the true and living Word of God that I have been encouraged to pen this letter to you. The Word of God says that He that is in you is greater than he who is in the world (I John 4:4, NKJV). So, upon my journey of discovering who He created me to be, I understand that I have dominion, freedom, and courage in Him. With this understanding, I have come to terms with being able to reflect on a few areas of my childhood and our relationship as mother and daughter that were once too painful to explore.

I understand you fled to Tacoma, Washington, to get away from my biological father after having me at age 21 in Virginia and suffering at the hands of his extreme physical and emotional abuse. What I remember being told about him is that he was an extremely tall man nicknamed '6' because he was over 6 feet tall. I understand that he was plagued by anxiety and PTSD after returning from the Vietnam War. Although I still have not met him, I am grateful that you got freed from him, persevered, and made sure I was with you and safe. That in itself is a miracle from God.

From the perspective of our Lord and Savior, I believe the enemy was trying to take me out of this world when I was in your womb and before God could make a miracle of the mess of a life I would ultimately create. The abuse you suffered was wrong and affected me deeply, although I was only 2 years old when you left. It has affected me in more ways than one through several seasons of my life. But it stops now. I no longer take hold of what the world says that aids in my harboring mistrust. I have laid down parts of nightmares I've had about how it may have happened that he was able to throw you from a moving car when I was in your belly and how he, as you said, smothered me with a pillow when I would scream when he came near my crib because I was terrified of him as a baby. At this point in my life, I cancel those burdens of hurt and distrust that tried to form and attach to what God ordained in me from the beginning. I can discern that the enemy was trying to take me out before I was even born and tried even harder when I was a baby. The caveat in this is that he still tried to take my life when I was shot 5 times in the stomach at the age of 18.

With all of this, I am so very grateful that you were able to develop the courage to leave, take me with you, and start a new life for the past 40 years with my now step-dad, who I adore just as deeply as I look upon you as my mother! I thank you, Mom, for saving my life. The Lord entrusted you with me, and you persevered and overcame. Thank you!

Some of the memories I had growing up in Tacoma include fighting with my cousins and envying some of them that ended up living with us through the years. I always felt like you had a better relationship with them than you did with me. I remember feeling like, *Why do they have to live here? They have their own parents, brothers, and sisters to play with.* I also remember that they were never required to clean up as much as I had to. I had to wash walls on Saturday mornings while Tawnya talked on the phone and hung out with you; that left me with feelings of abandonment, even though you and I were in the same home. You couldn't have known these were my feelings. I didn't know how to describe what I felt, and I would not have had the courage to tell you anyway; instead, I just reacted.

One of the most vivid memories I have of childhood is when I lived with Aunt Nancy and Kim in Washington, D.C. That is one of the clearest memories I have of my childhood. It was around this time that I was still in elementary school. I remember flying to D.C. with Aunt Nancy and being excited. When we arrived, I saw snow, which I had never seen before, and I was so excited. That was the last day I remember being the happiest while living with her. I played outside in shorts and didn't even feel cold. Everyone thought it was the cutest thing because I was from California, had never seen snow, and didn't have a clue that I needed to be covered in warm clothing.

Aunt Nancy lived in a small 2-bedroom apartment with my cousin Tony. The apartment was like a duplex, but there were three apartments within one huge building. That's the way they were made in North West, D.C. It was a dark building with barely any lights in the hallway. But what I remember being the best part about these living arrangements is that Aunt Nancy's daughter, my older cousin, and her two kids lived in the top apartment right up from us. I liked Kim; she was like my older cooler cousin. She had two kids that I loved to play with, and she wasn't always as strict as Aunt Nancy, but she was definitely not one to be tried and tested!

At this point in my childhood, I recall the constant feeling of anger and depression. I often exhibited volatile behavior, and that's why Aunt Nancy and Cousin Kim wanted me to receive help. I was taken to a facility within the Children's Hospital. At the age of 9, I was not only away from you as my mother, but I was also on the opposite coast from where you were and locked in a facility labeled as a troubled child. I felt lost, abandoned, very lonely, and with a sense of shame. The shame came from feeling like I was so bad I couldn't live with my mother and dad, nor could I live with my aunt. I knew Aunt Nancy and Kim loved me and were doing the best they could, making sure I was OK. But I could never figure out why I was there in D.C., and you were in California with Daddy. I think that was one of the times as a child I felt such intense emotions with no real ability to resolve or reflect on why I was feeling that way. It's still all not clear, but the associated feelings were such turmoil in my young life and still bring tears to my eyes today.

After about 23 years of that, I remember coming back home with you and Daddy to California. On the inside of my soul, I felt contention but had no outlet, so I took on the habit of running away a lot. One of the last times I ran away during this time, I remember being put in another facility similar to Children's Hospital, but it was worse and much more lonely. It felt like I was going to be away from you for good. I was about 11 or 12 years old at this time, almost the same age my daughter is right now. The loneliness and anger I felt melted my heart on a daily basis. This whole time was much of a blur. But I do remember getting a notice that you wouldn't be coming to see me because you were in rehab. Later, I found out that you had been entangled and suffering from the disease of alcoholism. At the time, I didn't really understand what that was or what it looked like. I don't even remember being affected by it. One of the only memories I had is when you would tell me each morning to go get you a bottle of beer out of the refrigerator. I vividly remember; it was a green bottle, and I would know it to be named Mickey's as I got older. So, in hindsight, you would drink Mickey's every morning. There would also be times when you would be really angry at Daddy. I recall one time you were so mad that you jumped up and down so hard that you ended up breaking your toe or foot or something. No one was hurt, but there were definitely times when you would be angry, and Daddy would retreat and try to get you to calm down. It's crazy how this same scenario played out in the beginning of my own now 15-year marriage … but we'll leave that story for the next book!

Still, at this point in my time in the facility, I only understood that you couldn't come to see me, and for some reason, Daddy didn't come to see me either. I can't remember how long it was, but it felt like an eternity. I can't remember what sent me into a rage, but I do recall consciously planning with another girl to run from that place too. Running was what I knew, and so I did it again. But this time, I ran. I called Auntie Carol. For some reason, though, she lived in Tacoma, Washington; I could always remember her telephone number. I called her, and she connected me to you, and you saved me.

I remember feeling so happy inside that my mother would be the one to pull me from this dark place and receive me like I had recently dreamed about. You were finally there to save me, to hold me, and to love me like the images I had about a mother and a daughter. So, you took me with you, and I never returned to that place again. It was the strangest thing. Even out of all of that goodness, the enemy still had a hold of the love God designed us to have for each other as mother and daughter. We were physically together. I was back with you and Daddy, but the emotional connection wasn't present. I do remember you trying. I recall us getting dressed alike, you being present while I started the 9th grade, and we lived well. We lived in a nice little house in Lawndale. The thing was, I was still being tormented on the inside with all of these feelings, all of the aspects of my life that had transpired up to this point.

I didn't know how to feel. I didn't know how to process emotions, the feeling of instability. Being with you both as a family was new; it seemed surreal. It seemed right on the surface, but I believe because we never processed or talked about anything that happened, the emotions were suppressed and were bound to come out, and they did. We didn't discuss the times I spent with the aunties, the rehab you went to, and certainly not my running away from this last facility or anything. I do recall you saying, "You can't run away. You can't get into trouble, or they'll take you back to that place." I was terrified at the thought of going back in my heart. But somehow, I couldn't roll with just picking up where we left off as a family all those years ago, so I started over. Things were good. But my inner man, the chaos within me, continued and worsened.

I understand you are the baby of all 12 of your siblings. I empathize with the fact that you lost your biological mother while you were just 2 years old. I realize why you may have used some of the strategies you did to raise me. I recall your explaining your feelings about never knowing your biological mother. I know you experienced even more death while raising me. Your dad passed, two brothers passed, and then eventually your step-mom that raised all of the 12 children also passed, leaving you and your seven sisters. Such trauma in our lives, unknowingly, often transfers to those we love the most. We don't know how to deal with such intense emotions at a young age, and as we grow, we see the remnants, the shattered pieces of things, and we try to put them back together, or we try to make sense of them, but without the light of the Lord our God, it remains a blur. I believe those same emotions connected with the circumstances of your childhood seeped into the depth of why our relationship started out with so many broken and missing pieces.

After not being able to put the pieces back together or even understand there were pieces that needed to be shaken off, reconfigured, and repositioned, the intensity of my inner turmoil and the curse of destruction swept me under. This time, and although I know in my heart you truly wanted to be there to save me from the next phase and challenges I would face in my life, you couldn't. It was too late to establish that bond between mother and daughter or the trust and intimacy of a relationship between child and parent. So, I was caught up. I got involved in the bigger world of destruction. I would be plunged into darkness for the next five years of my life that I actually contributed to, and it compounded the years of heartache I was already suffering from. My darkness would be deep, and no one could rescue me this time not you, Mom, and not even any of the aunties.

I remember in the 9th grade I was about 13 years old we settled in Lawndale, California, after several other smaller moves. I remember still having darkness in my spirit; the effects of everything that happened still pursued my emotional stability. Out of lack of self-control over my emotions, I would still habitually run away. Even though you and Daddy were showing me consistent love during this time, we had a wonderful family home and were building a foundation; I kept running and constantly fighting. As an only child and now a teenager, I found it hard to make friends. I quickly fell in with the wrong crowd, which included calling a notorious gang member my boyfriend. I do remember feeling lots of love and concern from you as my mother during this time of my life. I wanted so much to be at home and live a regular life, but my stubbornness had developed, and it was like I was attached to the darkness. Once again, my world, the parts that were slowly trying to be mended back together, began to slowly fall further and further apart.

I was sentenced to five years in the California Youth Authority. During the three years I served, I remember feeling lots of love from you and Daddy. You both were there for me. You both visited me every Sunday. You even would bring each of the aunties to visit me every so often. I think the whole time I was there, at least all seven aunties, though they lived in different parts of the world, visited me a few times each. It was an interesting time in my life, one in which the sadness didn't keep me down because I began to thrive in this place. I went to school; I was even part of the fire camp team that fought forest fires in Southern California. Though I was in a locked facility, looking back, I felt a presence of peace, self-discovery, and mostly of love—love from you and Daddy. This was definitely the part in my life that turned out to be a pivotal point of restoration not just for me but for our relationship as mother and daughter.

When I was released at age 16, you had moved to Carson, California. I remember coming home to the house you still live in today in Carson. You and Daddy had my room all fixed up, and I believe it was a purple or pink theme, one of those, but it was beautiful; it felt like a fairytale. Unfortunately, there were still hard times ahead for me. I constantly struggled with friends, school, and fitting in. Even in these struggles, I remember you being there like never before. It was great; there was a solid foundation established. There were regular house rules; it was just the three of us, but I just couldn't get it together. Whatever you and Daddy had gone through, you had preserved. Whatever happened with the alcoholism, you had been restored and redeemed; it was as if none if it ever happened. I never saw anything else in relation to the abuse of alcohol again; no more arguing or volatility, and there were even no other family members living with us. We went to church, we served, we were involved, and things seemed good. But me, well, I was still in deep darkness, and it began to seep out even more.

One of the biggest and most recent life lessons that I received from you is understanding that nothing is handed to you, not even from you as my mother. This is one of the honest truths I had to come to terms with. You lovingly warned me of truths growing up. One of the phrases you would always tell me is, "I'd be less than a mother not to tell you ..." That was what you would preface things with when you had to tell me the truth about something. It was helpful; it often softened the blow of whatever realization I had to face at the time. It was loving, and it was most always the truth. Still, this last lesson in my life and in our relationship was one of the toughest we've had hands down. The peace I get from it now is that God used it to strengthen me and teach me to continue to build. I now know that although James and I were supposed to buy the family business we helped build for more than 10 years and that you decided against it at the last minute, it worked out for the good of what the Lord had planned for our future.

At the time, your changing your decision would have been easier to swallow had it been before I quit my job as Director of the Domestic Violence Shelter. I was graced with a great position and a great boss at that time; I am actually still in touch with her today. But I remember we had gone through this same type of scenario before; this was the second time you had ultimately shut me out or 'laid me off,' as I was titled. That was a mess as well, but we got through it. But in this instance in 2015, I truly believed not just me but my husband and family had put in blood, sweat, tears, and time away from each other as a family for that business.

We knew in our heart that since I was your only child, had already helped build the business, and you were going to retire, we would continue the legacy. But even with all of that, you didn't select me to take it over or even buy it from you. I remember you even increased the price when we had agreed to a plethora of other outrageous terms. At the time, it felt as if you thought I couldn't do it, not even with the help of James. It felt as if you didn't even have a heart for how I worked so hard for you over the past years; how I sacrificed time with my family, my son when he was younger, and even had brought my husband to work in the business while he was working full-time. It ultimately felt like you thought I was not good enough. These feelings left me wounded for more than a year. It took me back to the times as a child where I felt no connection to you. I felt alone and as if I still didn't measure up. But perhaps it wasn't even about me; maybe it was just simply that you did not want to let go of the control.

The business was, in fact, what you had built over a span of 20 years from the ground up and after many other endeavors. Even though you had other jobs, you were always an entrepreneur since I was young. I remember you had a modeling agency, sold pantyhose, and then started your contracting business right after I went off to college while you were also working as a professor for a university. Who knew I would follow in those exact footsteps! Only God! But somehow, in His divine order, He stopped this pattern in its tracks. What almost turned my hearts inside out was used to propel me and my own family into a bigger and more blessed journey than we could have ever imagined. So, after finding out you didn't want me taking over the business, for me, in the innermost depths of my soul, it was one of the harshest blows to my heart and our relationship I had experienced in my adult life.

So, in 2016, after fasting for 21 days and discovering my purpose on earth was much large than my current circumstances, I felt the peace of God. With His peace and strength, I was able to pick up those shattered pieces, realizing that this was ultimately a pivotal shift, the beginning of a transformation in our family and in our own journey in business. The Lord makes us whole, and knowing and finally understanding that only HE loves us unconditionally, with an agape love that humans cannot even fathom, He then also qualifies us for what He wants and has called us to do. I realized maybe all this time, my dream to run the 'family business' was not in line with how He wanted me or my husband to proceed in business and that our journey and purpose together was going to be different. He used those circumstances to shape our future and made provision for us to establish a small business of our own. I felt heartache, but the Lord used it to begin a deeper healing process for me. He increased my drive and nurtured my gifts of development and administration. Ultimately, you, Mom, and all of the surrounding circumstances of this journey serve as part of the reason I was prepared for the challenge to start our business in the first place.

I know that there are missing pieces in this letter; it doesn't suffice for the complete picture of our relationship or who you are the wisest, most phenomenal woman I know. There were definitely times in my life that the brevity of these pages cannot cover, like the details associated with when I was riddled with bullets; in abusive relationships; and all through my undergraduate and graduate school experience where you were more than present, loving, and supportive in my life and in the life of my firstborn son. Our Lord God, you, and Daddy were all I had and the most consistent support and love I had as a young adult and newly single and divorced mother. Still, these portions of my story that I was able to reflect upon and explain are commensurate with how I felt like my life was full of shattered pieces that I had to find and, with the help of the Holy Spirit, put back together again.

Though I love you deeply, and I know you love me, there still remain fractured areas in our relationship punctured with levels of distrust and sadness that only God can continue to repair. The light and lesson is that the love of God in my heart lets me love you despite what we went through. It's because of our Lord and Savior Jesus Christ that I can now love in the face of trials and tribulations. It's not easy, but it's necessary. It's not perfect, but it's consistent. By His grace and mercy and with your help, Mom, I have overcome several major attacks on my life. I remain amazed at the revelation that our God continues to give us into situations of our past. Because God is the author of our stories and the finisher of our future, He gives us the dominion to change our circumstances, and I praise Him that I've been able to work on that with my own children and our relationships!

I want you to know, Mom, that these are just my memories, and they are in no way reflective of my love for you. I know it was hard for you in your childhood, and it was even more challenging to raise me after all that you continued to suffer and the circumstances that ended up being compounded into our relationship. The good news about our relationship is the promises of the Lord. He tells us in Revelation 3:20 that those who overcome will sit on the throne with Him when it's all said and done!

Relatedly, I have had similar feelings of grief, sorrow, abandonment, and deep saddening. I felt like some of the sporadic separation from you during those younger years of my life were like losing you. But now I can look at the situation or circumstances differently and with a new perspective. The hope comes from knowing my future is brighter than my past because God is the author and the finisher! So, when my daughter tells me these days, "You act like your mother," I often say to myself with warm confidence, *Yes, I am sort of like my mother. I was blessed with some of her awesome qualities.* But what's even more and the blessing in all of this is that I know in my heart that I am building and learning to be more like the image of Christ and the mother He wants me to be in a good and blessed way. This story is to be continued ... I love you, Mommie!

ABOUT THE AUTHOR

Deidre Norville is a Christian woman, a wife, and a mother of two biological children. She is a successful entrepreneur, professor in higher education, and served for more than a decade as Chief Operations Officer of community social welfare programs in Los Angeles, California. Deidre's unwavering passion for equality, diversity, and inclusion contributes to her transformative leadership style and her heart for service within the inner cities. Deidre received her bachelor's degree and then her master's degree in Social Work (MSW), with a focus on administration, policy, and planning, in 1999 from the University of Las Vegas, Nevada.

Deidre served as a Policy Professor for USC Suzanne Dwork Peck School of social work in the graduate program for 8 years. She also served as a member of the administrative team while simultaneously acquiring nearly a decade of experience and practice in community development and management of social welfare programs for parolees, homeless persons, and victims of domestic violence. Deidre also contributed to the arena of child welfare with the Los Angeles County Department of Children and Family Services, Adoptions Division, for nearly 5 years.

As an entrepreneur, Deidre and her husband own Norville Enterprises Inc. LLC, which serves as the umbrella for their family consulting and contracting business. Most recently, the couple built from the ground up OUR ESSENCE BEAUTY SUPPLY, which is a one-stop brick and mortar retail location for trending natural, vegan, and commercial hair and beauty products. The store incorporates a modernized customer service experience with consultation, education, on-site hair services, and beauty events for the community. In alignment with her transformative leadership style, Our Essence also serves as a small business incubator for smaller entrepreneurs that could seek to launch their businesses and products in a retail store that cannot get into big box spaces.

Over the decades, Deidre has been a member of the following associations and projects: University of California's Department of Social Work; Diversity Inclusion Committee; National California Partnership to End Domestic Violence; City of Los Angeles Emergency Food Services Program Executive Board; One Church One Child Adoption Initiative, American Correctional Association; National Correctional Industry Association; Southern California Minority Business Development Council; Light & Life Christian Fellowship Leadership Board; Chapel of Change Leadership Board; LLCF; Leadership research projects for the Center for Urban Research at California State, Dominguez Hills; Aid for AIDS of Nevada Strategic Planning Committee; Zeta Phi Beta Sorority, Incorporated; and By-Laws & National Policy Committee.

Deidre's life has been a motivation and a source of hope for others to reach and achieve more. She's demonstrated an abundance of perseverance through life struggles and continues to assist students, young professionals, and other women to be the best versions of themselves as already purposed by God. Deidre's prayer is that through the authentic sharing of her journey, the love of Christ shines so bright that it illuminates and touches the hearts of others so they, too, could come to know the hope and love of God!

Feel free to stay connected with Deidre Norville on social media at:

Instagram: http://www.instagram.com/professordeidre
LinkedIn: http://linkedin.com/in/deidrenorville
Store website: http://www.ouressencebeautysupply.com

Growing Pains

By:
Sara Johnson

From the wisdom that has left me and the ones that remain, this letter is written to you and to all moms that have growing women in their lives. I pour out prayers for the women that have been pressed to the wall. The women that give beyond their means out of sheer love. Overstretched moms that have changed roles and now serve as moms to their grandchildren. Moms that worked so hard building a legacy that somehow time surpassed moments that weren't supposed to be missed. Those that for one reason or the other couldn't love hard enough. I speak to you on a topic that each of us in some way has lived through and felt. That moment in time that generates a thin line of unanticipated tension lasting longer than intended. The pain of growing up and seeing that your little girl(s) no longer needs you to provide them with care from the sweat of your brow. She, however, desperately requires your wisdom and feminine union, that of a wholesome friend. This chapter speaks at that moment in our lives radiating with inconsistency, creating vulnerability upon both parties. However, if indeed viewed with the eyes of Proverbs 31, women, that vulnerability will turn into a distinguished opportunity.

A Grip of Resignation

I remember all so vividly as a little girl going through the process of growing up. I think I was about 13 years old, and I had gotten so mad at my mom because she embarrassed me in front of my friends. She slapped me right in front of two boys after giving her a crooked look to show that I didn't appreciate her bother. I was trying to be cute in front of them. However, I didn't know that she was looking and was too close for comfort. Not that I needed to do that in front of them because we grew up together. They knew that my mom wasn't mean; she just expected certain things from us. However, I dished that look to showcase power and control. She greeted me with a slap in the face that I have never forgotten. I was humiliated. I brought that disgrace on myself; however, it didn't matter I was mad! Not that my mother wanted to embarrass me, but she taught me a valuable lesson about denial.

While I didn't like what my mother did to me in front of my friends, on her end, she didn't like that I disrespect her in front of them. As a mother now, I appreciate that. Those young men are not in my life today. My mom, on the other hand, is still here! Today, I am humbled by that awful experience. It taught me the essence of regarding my mother when she's looking and not! As women, this is important. We require this of men, yet we often lack this quality with one another. Isn't that strange? We demand respect from a man in and out of our presence, while we trash another woman with no remorse. As moms and daughters, we have to do better. Seize the encounters endured together and sojourn emotional sufferings mutually so that you can heal and grow. Your story may be much worse than the one I provided, but that's okay. Every experience has a lesson that can be learned.

Stay Refined Together

While my mom was the one who humiliated me on that day, she still is with me. She still hears my cries and willingly wipes my tears. She begs for hugs from me, even though I hate to give them. When I need someone to talk to, she's there. Time is an essential element in a woman's life. We have so many levels of time that significantly impact who we are. For those that now miss this process of growth due to the end of a life cycle, I sincerely pray for you every day. My mom has lost her mother, so I see the pain you go through when no one is looking. I believe you can support me in stating, "Honor the time!"

We have a wonderful opportunity to be free in our self-expression. There have been so many men and women that have fought for this very liberty. Enjoy being a woman! Most of all, be willing to share this experience of liberty with your seed and your mom. Don't let time pass you. Love hard. Be free and bold. Work to build an honorable name. Embrace life together. Each of us wants to be heard and pampered. Duplicate the desire by being there for one another. The story of Naomi and Ruth is a perfect example of mothers and daughters growing up together with pride in their femininity. The respect that each had for the other embraced a strength that required respect. They were strong together. Time does help this process, yes, but generosity can as well. The respect that Ruth had for her mother-in-law did not develop overnight. Naomi fostered the wisdom of the Proverbs 31 woman. Her posture every day was a lifestyle that Ruth was willing to embrace. That says a lot about Naomi. Ruth gave up her culture and ways of living to connect with Naomi wholly.

In every woman's life, when it comes to becoming a woman and realizing that you now carry the torch of responsibility, pressure accumulates. Embracing mom delineates selfish imagery (that you may carry) of superiority and enriches the experience of living life together. A mom is never ready to let her princess go. Why should she accept you to force-feed your minimized view of her to her and not be affected by this depreciation? In the same sense, Mom, it's okay to say goodbye! One cannot purchase wisdom. It takes years of experience, slips, falls, bruises, and even slaps in the face to acquire.

Mom, don't hug so tight. Loosen your grip and let your swan fly. Show her how to love beyond the complexities of life. I believe that is how Naomi became so valuable in the eyes of Ruth. Naomi respected the fact that her time had expired on a level in Ruth's life. Now, that meant she had to face loneliness in the physical. There was a journey required of her. She would have to journey to her homeland and survive on her own. Coming to grips with her reality enabled her to accept her path. By doing so, she created a window of opportunity for Ruth to acknowledge her worth. Not only did Naomi need it, but she also yearned for the chance to thrive. They both were vulnerable in this situation, and yet, together, they each had a value that contributed to history.

Rooting for Both Sides

I know from experience that each side is precious and exposed. As daughters mature into women, Mom becomes a senior needing support. Both roles are significantly influential to the other. I genuinely believe it's how you capture the fragrance of both positions that advances the dynamic institution birthed as exhibited in the story of Ruth and Naomi. My mom has always been my best friend. I have told her the worst of the worst because I know she has my best interest at heart. She also drives me nuts and knows just how to get under my skin. However, no one else can do that to me. I do recognize that not everyone has that in their lives. Somewhere, somehow, some woman has been placed in your life to empower, enrich, and ignite the woman you are to be. God has put a gem in your sphere to build you in rare times. Embrace this treasure in the midst of your road.

An Open Heart

One of the things that I admire about my mom is that she has uncovered her heart to everyone she comes across. Her example is paramount. She's willing to contribute what she needs to produce. Available when the time is required. Even when we shut her off, as much as it hurts, she's active in saying, "Okay." Live your life, ladies, with an open heart. Be qualified to dispense what God has embedded within you but also have the wisdom to walk alone. It's easy to be selfish with who you are when you can't feel the entangled strings. Daughters, understand the pain of growing up, not under your skin but within your heart. Ruth felt the pain of walking away, but she loved her girls enough to let them grow up in a new world if they so desired. Naomi admired the wisdom of her mother-in-law in her actions, not through her words. I believe if both sides follow this example with exceptional balance, God will give the increase.

ABOUT THE AUTHOR

Originally from Baltimore, MD, Sara Johnson was the firstborn within the union of Elder Lee A. Andrew Johnson Sr. and Minister Tonya Johnson. One of eleven children, her childhood consists of strong Apostolic teaching from both her parents and her pastoral leaders. Her love for the ministry prospered by the robust influences of these great leaders: Bishop James Nelson Sr., the late Suff. Bishop Charles R. Brown, Apostle Cornelius Showell, District Elder Eugene King, Bishop Maxie Dobson, and Bishop Earnest Pendleton.

At the age of 8, Sara petitioned a mission to God. Giving her work over to the Lord, she aspired to be of service in His honor, not just on Sunday but every day of her life. The commitment was a heavy one to carry. The older she became, the deeper she felt the severity of living with a standard. Although inspired to share the gospel with her schoolmates, she found it easier to stand in the shadows and be average. Disappointed by her lack, she discovered liberty in working at church and writing. The urge to reach out did not die. Connecting her God-given talents and gifts into the working of the kingdom, she served within many areas of ministry, from youth leadership and Sunday school teaching to intercessory prayer and church administration. In addition to working with her hands within the vineyard, she dove into researching ministry structure and the use of the technology within the workplace.

Comprehending the need for technology integration within the ministry, Sara studied old manuals and electronic systems that could help bring the church into the 21st Century. She began connecting with Christian non-profits, like the Billy Graham Association, to feed her evangelistic appetite. Her writing increased, creating pieces for all occasions and soon became her mouthpiece. In 2009, she had the opportunity to work with Urban Believer Magazine and Girlz-In-Transition, becoming an officially published writer. As a contributing writer, she had a chance to write about gospel music, musical artists, specific topics inspiring young ladies, and health.

Today, Sara is also working on her degree in Evangelism at Liberty University. She has found her enjoyment in working from home, serving as a homeschooling parent, running her virtual office support business, and serving on multiple ministry platforms. Sara has connected her love of ministry to sharing what God has birthed in her through writing. This journey will premier with the 2019 publishing of her first devotion journal, *POSITIONED*, with a second in motion. She is also sharing in the delivery of *Dear Mom* as a contributing writer. While prepping her 15-year-old novel and motivational book for its upcoming publication for its entry into the hands of book lovers, she has found her cadence in the art world. Her theme and motivation have become her next two motivational pieces scheduled for publication in 2020.

Feel free to stay connected with Sara Johnson at virtual-yours@outlook.com

Feeding the Ducks

By:
Pam Murray

Dear Mom,

When I was a child, you would take me to Lake Carasaljo on Sunday afternoons after Mass. You would save scraps of bread all week, and we would feed the ducks. We would throw the bread, and the ducks would come running. We would throw the bread into the water, and the ducks would swim to get the bread. We would watch and laugh. Then we would go to what I can only describe as an amphitheater that had a stage where music would be played, and senior citizens would dance sometimes alone, and sometimes together. Sometimes you and I would sing and dance also. But most of all, we laughed. These were such happy times. As we watched the dancing, people seemed to be transformed.

They stood up straighter and smiled bigger. Suddenly, years and ailments and pain and trauma seemed to all melt away, and what was left in its place was joy pure joy. People were happy just dancing, singing, enjoying the music and each other's company.

We always managed to make our way to the lake, no matter what. You made sure of it. I suppose I get my love of music and dancing from you. You always seem to have a way with people. You talk to everybody. The 'gift of gab,' as it is called. I think I only got 20% of that. You have a good sense of humor. I definitely got that. You were standing up for yourself against the injustice that you faced at the workplace long before it was commonplace. You were fearless. I have always admired your drive, determination, and willingness to work hard. You started working on your bachelor's degree in 1976 when I was in the 6th grade. You got your degree in 1989 - 2 years after I graduated from the same university. You worked long hours. You had an almost 2-hour commute one way, and you had to be at work by 6 a.m. Amazing you managed to work, go to school, run a household, do homework, check on your own mother, mow the lawn, attend parent-teacher conference, and anything else I was involved in and still find time to feed the ducks. You found a way to get it all done and make it happen. After you retired, you spent countless hours not only planting and growing vegetables at the community garden but also harvesting them and delivering the produce to charities and churches. You even managed to teach Sunday school, sing in the choir, and be a cantor in your church. You worked at Great Adventure, at the polls, and as a home health aide. You volunteered to be an advocate for school-aged children. Even now, you still mow your lawn, rake your own leaves, cook and plant and harvest your own garden. All I can say is WOW!!

As I get older, I realize that 'feeding the ducks' really was not about feeding the ducks. Over the years, 'feeding the ducks' has been replaced with trips to Walmart or Cost-Co; apple-picking; taking walks; visiting friends; 'just driving around'; or sitting around, laughing. No matter what it is or what we do, it is still 'OUR THING.' It is what we do to stay connected. It is not the activity that is important because the activity or what you do can and will change. People get older; our bodies change; our minds change; interests change; people move away, get married, divorced, have children, or pass away. It is the connection to and with another person that matters. The only way to connect with someone is to not only spend time with that person but also to be present.

Spending time is different than spending 'quality time.' In our 'Facebook/Instagram' world, this sometimes does not happen, as people (myself included) are so much more interested in social media than in the human being sitting across from them. I am so grateful that I was raised in a time prior to social media where if you wanted to see someone, you had to leave your house, go to their house, knock on the door, and ask an adult if they were home. You would interact or connect if you wanted people in your life.

Mom, you taught me how to connect and genuinely enjoy people (most of the time). Being connected keeps us alive and healthy. I have learned that these connections lay the foundation for relationships. Relationships lead to feelings of well-being, confidence, and value. When we know we are valuable and appreciated, it fosters our expression of individuality. When we learn to embrace our differences, it is a source of strength and faith.

How could I not be great with having you as an example? How could I not be who I am? Strong-willed, driven, and compassionate. This is what makes us better friends, better parents, better employees, and overall better people. This has never been more evident in my life as now, as I am looking for a new job. At 53 years old, with many years of experience, it has not been easy to find employment. Although everyone says that nurses are in demand, I am finding that not to be the case.

I would like to thank you for all of your support and encouragement over the years and for your never-ending belief in me and my abilities. Thank you for always seeing the best in me, even when I was presenting you with the worst.

Thank you for your example and for showing me what someone can do if they just put their mind to it and don't give up.

Your concept of motherhood is to be present be there in good times to acknowledge and praise and, in bad times, not to judge but to encourage, support, and uplift. This has brought me to where I am today, and I am forever grateful. If I can attain just 1/8th of who you are, trust me, the world is a better place.

So, to everyone reading this book, take a lesson from Vandella no matter what station in life you find yourself, whether the sea of life is turbulent and you're are being tossed here and there, or if the waters are calm, go feed the ducks. Your very life depends on it.

ABOUT THE AUTHOR

Pam Murray was born in New York and moved to New Jersey at the age of 5. She received a Bachelor of Arts degree from New York University, a Bachelor of Science degree from the College of Saint Elizabeth, and a master's degree in Public Administration. She hopes to return to NYU to complete the Nurse Practitioner program. She works as a Unit Manager at a Nursing Home in New York. She enjoys crochet, dancing, and going on boat rides.

Pam is also a contributing author of Dear Dad, which is an Amazon Best Seller.

Feel free to stay connected with Pam Murray at SistahPam@gmail.com.

Carrying The Paton

By:
Vanessa Canteberry

Dear Mom,

Often times I wondered if you would ever be proud of me not just for my accomplishments but just being your daughter who stepped out to break the dysfunction in the way she was raised by showing her children a better way. Never in my wildest dreams would I ever have imagined that you never loved me. I accepted that you had a hard time expressing it.

I would think back to the time when you would have conversations about your childhood, and I would see the pain in your eyes until the point where you would never finish the story. I had to dig deeper into the history of your story to get a better understanding of how I make a better story for myself.

Your story carried trauma, pain, and so much more your entire life, and in return, your brokenness was on display. The brokenness kept you away because the healing was too much of a nightmare to relive. Unfortunately, memories couldn't be created because it was such a blur.

Reflecting on a conversation during which you asked me if I wrote about my father in the *Dear Dad* book, and I said yes. At that same moment, I told you about this book and that I would be writing about you as well. You looked at me in shock and automatically assumed I was going to air the brokenness of our relationship. However, in reality, I needed to introduce you to someone you didn't know—me.

My vision is not to throw you away and misplace the key. Rather, my mission is to bring awareness to many who may be going through the trauma of our experience, giving them a better outlook on life. When I told you before that I forgave my parents, I actually did. It's not in my place to say if there should be punishment for the things that happened to me. That's totally up to God. I know I needed to work on myself so as not to repeat the same behavior I exhibited. This is the person you didn't give a chance to know.

Do you remember the conversation we had when I braided your hair? I asked you, "Do you feel as if you are a broken woman?" With tears in your eyes, you replied, "Yes."

I said, "I am not here to beat you down; I am here to have a conversation with you." I am a believer that healing begins from having a conversation, and since we don't see each other often, let alone have a lengthy conversation, God made time for the moment to take place.

You proceed to tell me you are the middle child. I knew what that meant, but I wanted to hear it from you. You couldn't answer, so I continued to provide you an insight into being the middle child. "You see, Mom, I am also a middle child. I, too, had three children at the age of 21 and divorced when I was 24." You looked at me as tears rolled down your face. I then said to you, "Now, do you see there was something wrong with repeating the same cycle of dysfunction? I had no other choice but to find a better way because my children are looking at me to be their role model."

We both experience mental, physical, and emotional abuse. We can both relate, but the difference is, one is willing to sit in her pain to learn how to not return, while the other continues to hold onto the pain, and now it's become poison to her offspring.

Don't be mad at me because I left the comfort zone of brokenness. I hope that one day you will genuinely find wholeness in your heart to forgive those individuals who got you so broken.

Your grandchildren and great-grandchildren experience a life of transformation due to me doing the work to not repeat what was already broken but to seek healing in becoming whole so I can show them better. God is amazing!

Deep down inside, when you had your good days, they were amazing. Even if it was for a moment of the day, I cherished it and thought of how I could recreate such moments to create memories with my own children.

You taught me so much without even teaching me. I had to evaluate my own brokenness and step into a place of pain in order to forgive. It was not easy, but it was necessary because I was determined to finally put an end to the repeated cycles and exposed it in a negative light.

When I look at my children, I thank myself for not giving up on me. I had to learn a new behavior compared to what I saw.

I thank you for keeping me when you could have aborted me, especially when you were in the most devastating place in your life at the time you gave birth to me. God revealed to you that a miracle was being born at the time of my delivery, and who would have ever expected that her name would be Vanessa Canteberry? I thank you for showing me what not to do while raising my children. I thank you for the moment of silence that allowed me to learn more about God. Thank you for covering me to the best of your ability.

Mom, your first daughter found her own identity and made something of herself. She raised her children as a single parent and did an amazing job, I may say. It's not my place to punish you for not having the strength to fight harder. My prayer for you is that you find forgiveness and peace. Above all, God protected you when many wanted to destroy you. When it's all said and done, you, too, are a survivor.

Love always,

Your daughter

ABOUT THE AUTHOR

Vanessa Canteberry is the CEO of InspiredByVanessa. She was born and raised in Chicago, Illinois. She's determined to continue to break the cycle of poverty, negligent, and unnecessary hardship. Vanessa worked in Corporate America for 20 years as a Secretary. After being laid off in 2011, she knew something needed to change, knowing she was a single parent of three. Vanessa was not able to obtain employment, and the mere thought of being unable to support her son attending high school and two daughters attending college was unbearable.

For that reason, Vanessa challenged herself. She took a stand on faith and changed her mindset. She's on a mission to educating individuals on the importance of transformation of the W2 mindset in life and business.

She's also is the business owner of Breaking Barriers Unapologetically and co-host of Motivate Social Podcast. Vanessa is a Speaker, Mindset Coach, Self Published 7 times Best Selling Author, working from the comfort of her home. She is also committed to teaching individuals how they, too, can become a business owner and overcome obstacles in their life.

Your past does not determine your destiny; make what seems impossible possible. InspiredByVanessa stands on FAITH and refuses to allow FEAR to void VISIONS that need to be seen and heard on so many platforms. She teaches you that you are more than a W2.

Vanessa is the Best Selling Author of Shifting Your Mindset and Breaking the Cycle of Brokenness, Co-Author I Am More Than, Do I Not Matter and the Compiler for the anthology Screams of a Broken Woman and Cries of a Broken Man, Dear Dad and Dear Mom.

Feel free to stay connected with Vanessa Canteberry on social media at:

www.Facebook.com/InspireVanessa

www.Instagram.com/InspiredByVanessa
www.Twitter.com/InspireVanessa
www.LinkedIn.com/in/VanessaCanteberry
http://www.InspiredByVanessa.com

Acknowledgment

To all the authors, from the bottom of my heart, I say thank you. Thank you for sharing your transparent stories of your moms. Some may have been easier than others, but still, in all, we are helping somebody else with our stories.

Thank you for trusting the vision of this collaboration God has given me. I will be forever grateful.

Much respect,

Vanessa Canteberry

www.ingramcontent.com/pod-product-compliance
Lightning Source LLC
Chambersburg PA
CBHW030813090426
42736CB00027B/581